CLOCKS
AND TIME

Ed Catherall

Wayland

Young Scientist

First published in 1982 by Wayland (Publishers) Limited
49 Lansdowne Place, Hove, East Sussex BN3 1HF, England
© Copyright 1982 Wayland (Publishers) Limited
ISBN 0 85340 912 9

Designed and illustrated by Chris Smithers
Typeset by Plus 5 Limited, London
Printed in Italy by G. Canale & C. S.p.A., Turin

Contents

Chapter 1 Early timekeepers

Clocks and time

At what time do you get up on school days?
When do you leave for school?
When does school start?

What is your favourite lesson?
How long is your favourite lesson?
Which lesson do you dislike most?
How long is this lesson? Do you often look
at a clock during this lesson?
Does time appear to go as fast during
a lesson that you dislike as it does
during one that you like?

What sporting records do you know?
How much time did these speed records take?
How was the time measured?

How many watches, clocks and other
timers are there in your house?

Make a scrapbook of pictures of all sorts
of clocks, watches and timers. Label your
pictures and add any information that you
discover

A clock is, by definition, a mechanical instrument
which *strikes* to indicate time.
The name comes from the old English word
clokke, or clok, which means bell.
Are there any striking clocks in your house?
In this book, we will use the word clock, as most
people do, to mean a timekeeper.

Shadows

Why do you think people needed to measure time?
One reason given by historians is that humans needed to know when to carry out religious rites and other important group gatherings.

Go outside on a sunny day.
In what general direction is the sun?
Do not look directly at the sun as it will damage your eyes.
Why doesn't everyone in the world see the sun in the same general direction as you do?
How long is your shadow?
Ask a friend to draw around your shadow on the ground.

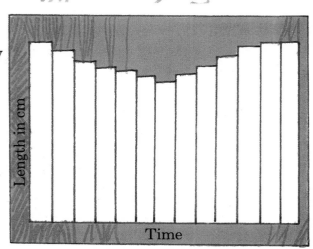

Go outside one hour later.
Stand in the same place.
What has happened to your shadow?
Why is your shadow different?

Place a stick upright in the ground.
Mark the position of the shadow every hour, on the hour.
What do you notice about the length of the shadow?
When is the shadow shortest?
Why is this?
Draw your shadows to scale and make a histogram of them.

Length in cm

Time

Shadow sticks

Old churches in Europe often have a hole in the wall near the door.
There are scratch marks radiating from the hole.
A stick was placed in the hole and when the shadow fell on a scratch mark it was time for a church service to start.

Find a vertical pole, such as a flagpole.
Measure the shadows that this pole makes on the hour at different times of the year.
Draw your shadows to scale.
Carefully record the angles of the shadows and date them.
What do you notice when you compare shadows several months apart?
What does this tell you about the length of the day and the position of the sun?

Try to measure the *exact* time every day when the pole has the shortest shadow. Notice how your results vary.

Summer shadows

Winter shadows

17·00
16·00
15·00

12·00
9·00
10·00
11·00
13·00
14·00
15·00
9·00

Making a model Egyptian shadow clock

Find a length of thick wood or a long cardboard box, like those used to hold metal foil.
Fix a pencil across the top of the box with sticky tape.

Take your shadow clock outside on a sunny day. Early morning or late afternoon is the best time.
Place a sheet of paper on a flat, horizontal surface.
Put your shadow clock on the paper.
Point your shadow clock towards the sun. Check that the shadow of the box is directly behind the box.
Look down on the top of your shadow stick. Where do you see the shadow of the pencil?

On the hour, mark the position of the shadow on the top of your box.
Always point your shadow clock directly towards the sun.
Are the hour-markings evenly spaced?
In which direction does the shadow move in the morning?
In which direction does the shadow move in the afternoon?
Do the morning and afternoon hours match?

Around 700 B.C., the Egyptians used portable shadow clocks.
These clocks had five hour-lines plus the midday line.

Making a sundial

If you see a sundial, make a drawing of it to add to your scrapbook.

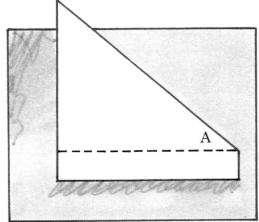

Look in an atlas to find the latitude of your town.
Look at the shape in the picture on the right.
Draw two similar shapes on thick cardboard.
Make the angle A the same as your latitude.
Cut out and fix these shapes back-to-back with glue or sticky tape.
These shapes act as the gnomon or shadow marker of your sundial.
The angle A is the same as your latitude so that your gnomon is parallel to the axis of the Earth.

Draw a half-circle on a wooden base.
Fix your gnomon onto the wooden base.
Place your sundial on a flat surface in the sun. Set your gnomon so that it points north and south.
Mark the position of the sun on the half-circle every hour, on the hour. Notice that the shadow moves at a uniform rate.

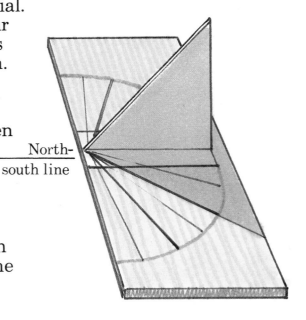

North-south line

If you want your sundial to withstand rain, make your gnomon of wood or strong plastic.

Making a water clock

The early Greeks and Egyptians used a clepsydra, or water clock, to measure time.
Clepsydra is a Greek word meaning water thief.

Use a hammer and a nail to punch a small hole in the base of a large, empty can.
Put your finger over the hole and fill the can with water.
How long does the can take to empty?
Mark the water level every minute.
Does the water level fall at a steady rate?

Put your empty can upright in a large container of water.
How long does it take for the can to sink?
Does it take the same amount of time to sink as it did to empty?
Mark the water level every minute. Does it sink at a steady rate?
What do you notice about the emptying marks and the sinking marks?

Weight the can with washers.
Record the effect of the weight on the time taken to sink the can.
Record your results.

Number of washers	Time taken for can to sink

Try to make a clepsydra that takes exactly 15 minutes to empty.
Mark the minutes on the side of your clepsydra.

Making a model Chinese water clock

Find six identical clean plastic cartons.
Make a small hole in the middle of the base of five cartons.
Mark a centimetre scale on the side of the sixth carton.

Screw the five cartons with the holes in their bases, one above the other, onto a board.
Place the carton with the scale under the other five.

Put your finger over the hole in the top carton. Fill the top carton with water.
How long does it take for the first drops of water to reach the bottom carton?
How long does it take for the water level in the bottom carton to reach 1 cm?

Mark the bottom carton with a time scale.
How can you make your clock go faster?
What happens if you put a little liquid detergent in the water?

The Chinese also made water clocks using water wheels.
Find out how these clocks worked.

10

Making a sand clock

Find a clean, dry plastic bottle and a clean, dry glass jar.
See that your bottle will rest upside down in the neck of the jar.
Find some dry sand. Sift the sand to remove any large particles.
You can use salt instead of sand.

Check that there is only a small hole in the top of the plastic bottle.
If not, make a small hole in the cap of the bottle.
Cut the base off the bottle.
Fill the bottle with sand.
Fit the bottle upside down into the neck of the jar.
How long does it take for the bottle to empty completely?

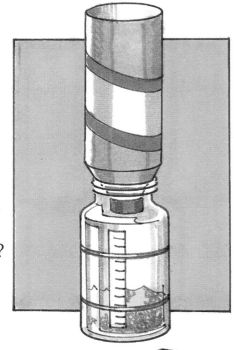

Make a paper scale. Fix your scale to the outside of the jar with rubber bands.
How long does it take for the sand to reach each mark on your scale?
Remember to read the pile of sand in the same way each time.
Does the sand fill the jar at a steady rate?
Can you make a scale that will measure minutes?
Use your sand clock to time things.

Have you ever seen a sand clock?
What was it used for?

In the past, sand clocks were often mounted in fours. One measured 15 minutes, one 30 minutes, one 45 minutes and one the hour.

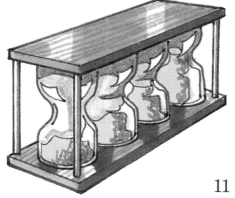

Candle clocks

You must ask an adult to help you make candle clocks.
Measure the length of a candle.
Use a large lump of modelling clay to fix the candle in the middle of a large, flat metal dish or lid.
Place the dish in the middle of a large metal tray. Surround the dish with a layer of sand.

Light the wick of the candle.

Make sure that you do not bend over the candle. Be certain that your hair and clothes are not near the candle flame.
After an hour, blow out the candle flame. When the candle is cold, measure it again. How much shorter is the candle after it has been burning for 1 hour?
How many hours of burning are left in the candle?
With a pin, scratch half-hour distances along the candle.

Relight your candle. Look at your candle every half-hour.
How accurate were your marks?

Try using other candles. Do all candles burn at the same rate?

King Alfred, a Saxon king of England, used candle clocks.
His candle had hour-markings on it and was kept in a lantern to protect it from wind.

Chapter 2   Mechanical clocks

A skittle game

Place two chairs back-to-back.
Place a stick across the chairs
to form a bridge. Tie a string to
the middle of the stick. Fix a ball
of modelling clay to the end of
the string.
You have made a pendulum.

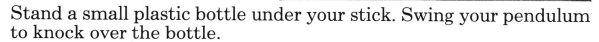

Stand a small plastic bottle under your stick. Swing your pendulum
to knock over the bottle.

Find nine empty match boxes or nine tall corks to act as skittles.
A short pencil pushed into each cork will make the skittles taller.
Stand a stick upright in the ground in front of a flat area.
Tie a length of string to the top of the
stick. Tape the string in place. Make a
pendulum bob with a ball of modelling clay.

Stand your skittles on the flat surface
behind the stick. Arrange the skittles in
a triangular pattern.
Check to see that your pendulum can
reach each skittle.
Swing your pendulum in a circle around
the stick.
How many skittles can you knock down
with one swing?

Make up a skittle game with your friend.
How many skittles can you knock over
in three swings of the pendulum?
Reset the skittles if you knock them all
over in less than three swings.

Arrange your skittles in different patterns to vary the game.

13

A pendulum

Make a hook from a wire paperclip. Tape the hook
to the middle of a doorway arch.
Fix a small ball of modelling clay to the end of a
length of thread.
Push a pin into the ball of clay to act as a marker.
Tie the thread to the hook so that the pin almost
touches the ground.
You have made a pendulum.

Cut a long length of paper.
Mark the paper in centimetres,
starting from the middle of the
doorway arch.

Release your pendulum in a
straight line over the paper.
Record the distance at which
you start the swing.
Does your pendulum return to
this point?
Record the distance the
pendulum bob reaches on each
swing.
What do you notice about this
distance?

Release your pendulum from a
greater distance. Record the
distance of each swing.
What do you notice?

Next time you are on a swing,
notice what you have to do to
work the swing. What happens
when you stop working?

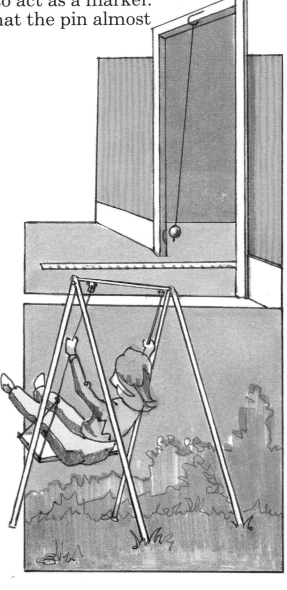

14

What makes a pendulum stop swinging?

Cut out two squares of cardboard, each 5 cm by 5 cm. Cut a 2·5-cm slit in each card.
Fix the two cardboard squares together to form a cross. Tape the squares to strengthen the cross.
Tape a length of thread to the top of the cross to make a pendulum.
Use modelling clay to fix a pin to the base of the cross.
Use this pendulum to repeat the experiment on page 14.

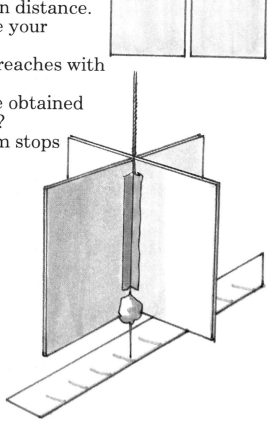

Release your pendulum from a known distance.
Record the time at which you release your pendulum.
Record the distance your pendulum reaches with each swing.
How do your results differ from those obtained with a modelling-clay pendulum bob?
Record the time when your pendulum stops swinging.

Cut out another two cardboard squares, each 10 cm by 10 cm.
Make these squares into a cross.
Repeat the experiment using this larger cross.
Does this pendulum swing as far as the one with the smaller cross?
Does this pendulum stop more quickly?
What happens if you make an even larger cross?
What do you think is slowing down your pendulum?
What happens if you blow on your pendulum?

The effect of the weight of a pendulum bob

Fix two hooks to a doorway arch so that two pendulums can swing side by side.
Cut two equal lengths of thread.
Use sticky tape to attach a table tennis ball to one thread.
Make a modelling-clay ball the same size as the table tennis ball.
Fix the clay ball to the other thread.
Lift each pendulum. Which is heavier?

Tie the threads to separate hooks in the doorway.
Check that both pendulums hang down equally.

Release both pendulums in a straight line.
Make sure that you release both pendulums from the same distance and at the same time.
What happens?
Do both pendulums return to the same mark?
Which pendulum stops swinging first?

Repeat the experiment from different distances.
What results do you get?
Does the weight of the pendulum bob affect the swing?

Timing with a pendulum

Set up this experiment similar to the one on page 14. As you will be shortening your pendulum, pass the long thread of the pendulum through the hook and tape the end to the door frame.
Measure the length of the thread from the hook to the bottom of the clay bob.
Adjust the length until it is an exact number of centimetres.

Release the pendulum.
Record the time of release.
Record the time taken for forty swings.

Shorten the length of the pendulum by 10 cm.
Release the pendulum.
Record the time taken for forty swings.
Is this time less?

Keep shortening your pendulum by 10 cm.
Record the time for forty swings.
Graph your results on squared paper.
What length of pendulum will take 40 seconds to make forty swings? Make a pendulum of this length.
Does this pendulum take 1 second to make one swing?

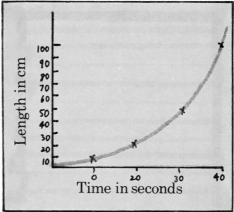

Time forty wide swings and forty narrow swings.
Does the size of the swing alter the time taken by the pendulum?

In 1582, Galileo watched a lamp swinging in Pisa Cathedral, and decided that wide swings and narrow swings took the same time.
In fact, very large swings take slightly longer than small swings.

Pendulum patterns

Find a clean, dry plastic bottle which has a nozzle on the top. A washing-up liquid bottle is ideal.
Remove the nozzle.

Make a hole in the middle of the base of the bottle. Thread string through this hole and through the hole in the top. Tie a matchstick to the string.
Put the matchstick into the bottle.
Hold up your bottle by the string.
Tie the string to a stick fastened across the backs of two chairs (see page 13).
Check that the bottle hangs just above the floor.

Place a large sheet of paper on the floor under your pendulum.
Pour a cupful of salt or sand into the bottle and replace the nozzle.
Swing your bottle in a small circle.
What pattern do you make?
What other patterns can you make?

You can make permanent patterns on paper covered with a layer of wet wallpaper paste.

Find eight identical plastic tubs. Put these tubs in a line under your swinging bottle.
Which tub is filled with the most salt or sand?
Which tub is filled with the least salt or sand?
What does this tell you about the swing of a pendulum?

Double-suspension pendulums

Make a salt or sand pendulum (see page 18).
Suspend your pendulum from two places on your support stick. What pattern do you make?

Change the length of strings A and B.
What happens?
Change the distance apart of strings A and B.
What happens?
What happens if you make strings A and B of different lengths?

Find a long knitting needle.
Wind strings A and B around the knitting needle.
Put equal-sized balls of modelling clay on both ends of the knitting needle.
What pattern does your salt or sand pendulum make?

What happens if you slant your knitting needle by making strings A and B of different lengths?

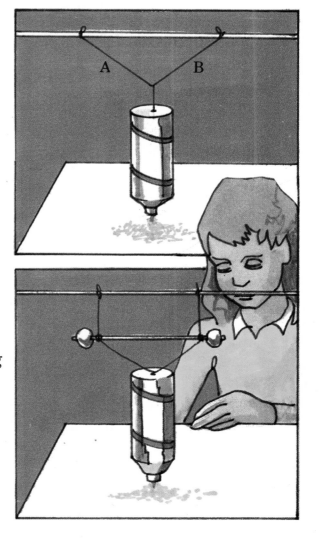

What pattern do you get if you increase the amount of modelling clay on each end of the needle?
What pattern do you get if you have a large clay ball at one end and a small one at the other end?
Watch carefully while the pattern is being made, and try to find out why you get a particular pattern.

19

Joined pendulums

Suspend two modelling-clay
pendulum bobs side by side from
a doorway arch (see page 16).
Wind the string of each of your
pendulums the same way around
a horizontal wooden rod.
Hold one pendulum bob still and
set the other swinging.
Release the pendulum bob that
you are holding. Be sure not to
swing this bob as you release it.
What happens?

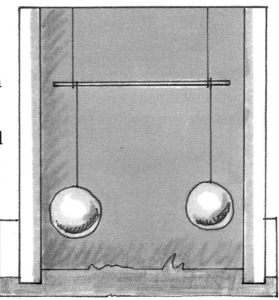

Raise the wooden rod. Repeat
this experiment.
What happens?
Lower the wooden rod. Repeat
this experiment.
What happens?
What happens if the rod is
slanted?
What happens if you make one
pendulum bob heavier than the
other?

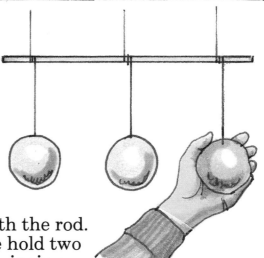

Join three pendulums together with the rod.
Repeat the experiment. This time hold two
pendulum bobs still while one is swinging.
Then release the other two together.
What happens if the swinging bob is at one end?
What happens if the swinging bob is in the middle?
What happens if you swing two pendulum bobs
and hold one still?

Driving a pendulum clock

There are many kinds of pendulum clocks.
Grandfather clocks are driven by a weight.
This moves the hands around the clock face.
The clock also has to have a regulator to
keep the hands moving at a constant speed.
The pendulum in the grandfather
clock acts as a regulator, as it
makes one swing each second.
The swinging pendulum and the
drive for the hands are linked by
an escape wheel on the drive,
and by an escapement on the
pendulum.

Escape wheel

Draw an escape wheel on thick
cardboard.
Cut out the wheel and glue it to
a cotton reel or thread spool.
Attach a hook made from a
paperclip to the end of a thread
wound around the cotton reel.
Weight the hook with washers.

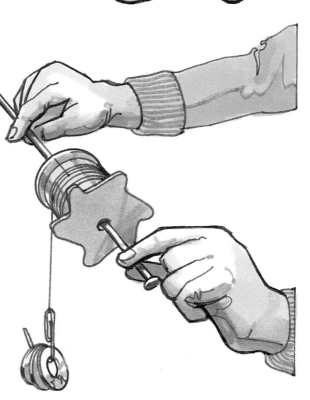

Put a knitting needle through
the middle of the cotton reel and
the escape wheel.

Hold the knitting needle and
watch the hook unwind. Notice
how this unwinding turns the
cotton reel with its escape wheel.
If you fixed a pointer to the
cotton reel, it would move like
one of the hands on a clock face.
Adjust the weight so that your
escape wheel turns slowly and evenly.

Regulating a pendulum clock

A clock needs to be regulated so that the hands of the clock move once every second. Draw an escapement and a narrow pendulum on thick cardboard.
Make sure your escape wheel (see page 21) fits inside the pallets on the escapement.
For a pendulum to make one swing every second, it should be 99.2 cm long (see page 17).
Cut out the escapement and pendulum. Attach a weight to the end of your pendulum.
Push a knitting needle through the hole in the escapement.

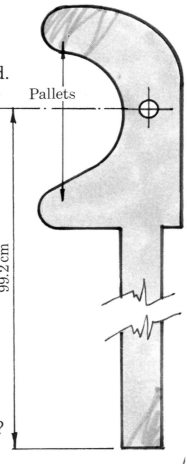

Pallets

99.2 cm

Swing your pendulum. Notice how the pallets on the escapement nod up and down with each swing of the pendulum. Does your pendulum swing once a second? Does your escapement nod once a second? You have made a pendulum-clock regulator.

Ask a friend to hold the knitting needle which holds the pendulum.
You hold the knitting needle which is connected to your driving mechanism and escape wheel (see page 21).
Engage your escape wheel inside the escapement. What happens?
Ask your friend to swing the pendulum. Try to get your escape wheel to turn one cog with each swing of the pendulum.

Vibrating and atomic clocks

Modern clocks and watches are not driven by a falling weight. Usually, an uncoiling spring or an electric motor drives them. Modern clocks are not regulated by a pendulum.

Make a salt or sand pendulum (see page 18). Place a large sheet of paper under your pendulum. Swing your pendulum sideways with small swings. Pull the paper towards you evenly while the pendulum is swinging. What pattern do you get? What happens to the pattern if you alter the speed at which you pull the paper?

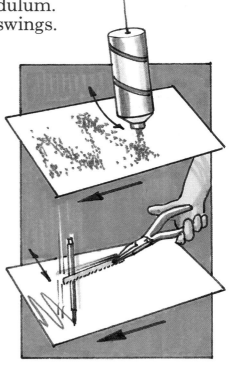

Use sticky tape to fix a felt-tip pen to the end of a springy hacksaw blade. Hold the other end of the blade with a pair of pliers. Lightly rest the pen on a piece of paper. Ask a friend to slowly pull the paper while you vibrate the blade. What pattern do you get? Is the pattern similar to the one made by the salt pendulum? You could repeat this experiment using a tuning fork instead of the saw blade.

Some modern watches use a vibrating tuning fork as a regulator, because a tuning fork gives a constant vibration.

A quartz crystal can be used as an accurate regulator, since it will vibrate at a constant radio frequency.

Atomic clocks use the natural vibration of the caesium atom. An atomic caesium clock is guaranteed not to lose even 1 second in 100,000 years.

Making a rolling-ball clock

Make a slope using a sheet of thick
cardboard.
Let a marble roll down the slope.
Alter your slope. Which slope does it take
your marble the longest time to roll down?

Measure the diameter of your marble.
Cut several strips of cardboard, each
twice as wide as the diameter of your
marble.
Fold each cardboard strip in half along
its length to make a trough.
You may need to score the back of the
cardboard to make it easier to fold.

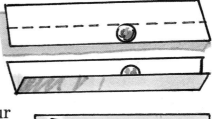

Hold one of your troughs at an angle.
See that your marble rolls down the
trough slowly. Use sticky tape to fix your
cardboard trough to a sheet of cardboard.
Fix your other troughs to the cardboard,
so that when your marble leaves one
trough it starts rolling down the next.
Can you arrange your troughs so that
your marble takes exactly 10 seconds to go
from start to finish?
You have made a 10-second regulator for
a clock.

Galileo invented the first rolling-ball clock.
William Congreve (1772-1828) made many rolling-ball clocks. In his
clocks, a ball took 30 seconds to reach the end. Then the base tilted
the other way allowing the ball to start again.

Chapter 3   Astronomical clocks

Units of time

At what time did the sun rise today?
At what time will the sun set today?
So, at what exact time is midday?
Record the times of sunrise and sunset
each day for many days.
Make a graph of these times.
Mark the midday point each day.
This midday point is the time you have
the shortest shadow.

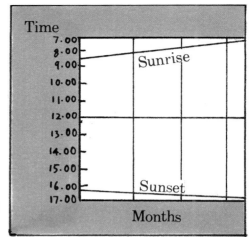

How long is the shortest day on your graph?
Divide this day into twelve equal parts.
How long is each 'sun hour'?
How long is the longest day on your graph?
Divide this day into twelve equal parts.
How much longer is this 'sun hour'?
Early man calculated his hours in this way.
Notice how the length of each 'sun hour'
varies from day to day.

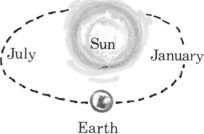

We say that the Earth takes 24 hours to rotate
once on its axis. From this, we calculate the length
of 1 hour, and then we calculate the minutes and
seconds.

The Earth follows an elliptical path around the
sun. This brings the Earth closest to the sun in
January and farthest from the sun in July.
When the Earth is closest to the sun, the sun's
gravitational pull makes the Earth rotate faster.
So, one rotation of the Earth in January is about
15 seconds faster than one rotation of the Earth
in July.
For our clocks, we just use the average time.

25

Time zones

The Earth rotates from west to east once every 24 hours.
There are 360° of longitude, so the Earth rotates through 15° of longitude every hour.
Each 15° of longitude is a time zone, and each zone differs from the next by 1 hour.

The sun appears to be directly overhead at midday. The Earth's rotation makes midday 1 hour different for each 15° of longitude.

For historical reasons, longitude was measured from Greenwich, England, and so time is measured from noon in Greenwich.
This time is called Greenwich Mean Time, G.M.T.

Look in an atlas to find the longitude of your town.
What time is it in your town?
What time is it 15° west of you?
What time is it in the Greenland time zone?
What time is it in the Pacific time zone?
What time is it in Delhi, India?
What time is it in Tokyo, Japan?
What kind of shadow would you expect from a shadow stick in New York, U.S.A. and Cape Town, South Africa now? (See page 6.)

Longitude

Time zones

Many countries have more than one time zone.
The boundaries between time zones are altered to avoid passing through large towns. Where is the International Date Line?

Star time

Find a stick about 1·5 metres long.
Screw an eye screw into the top of the stick.
Stand the stick upright in a can of earth.

On a clear night, take your stick outside.
Use a star map to identify the
constellations.
Look through the eye screw. Move the
stick until you can line up a star with the
top of a tree, pole or house.
At regular intervals, look at your star
through the eye screw. Does the star
appear to move?
Check several stars. Do they all move?
If you live in the northern hemisphere,
check to see if the North Star moves.

Draw a circle on paper. Mark the position
of the North Star in the middle.
At hourly intervals mark the position of a
constellation. Notice how the constellation
appears to revolve around the North Star.
Constellations appear to revolve around
the North Star because we are observing
them from the rotating Earth.

Use your circle as a star clock.
If you do this experiment over several weeks, you will notice that
your stars appear at different places on your star clock.
This is because we time the rotation of the Earth from the sun.
As we are also revolving around the sun, it takes 4 minutes longer
each day for the sun to appear overhead.
Star time tells us that one rotation of the Earth takes 23 hours
56 minutes.

The calendar

A year is the length of time that the Earth takes to revolve around the sun.

A year is 365 days, 5 hours, 48 minutes and 46 seconds. This creates two problems. How do we divide the 365 days into months? What do we do with the extra 5 hours 48 minutes and 46 seconds?

Julius Caesar's calendar had a leap year every four years, and Augustus Caesar kept this system. This meant that each year was 11 minutes and 14 seconds too long.

Over the years this added up, and in 1582 Pope Gregory found that the spring equinox, which had been on 21 March in A.D. 325, was on 11 March in 1582. Therefore, 10 days had to be removed. In Britain, the calendar was not adjusted until 1752, by which time 11 days had to be removed. To correct this, there is a leap year every four years, but not in the century years, unless they can be evenly divided by 400. The next century leap year will be in A.D. 2000.

Find out about calendars of different religions and races. When is their New Year?

Julius Caesar's calendar, 46 B.C.

First	Second	Third	Fourth
31 days	29 days	31 days	30 days
Fifth	**Sixth**	**Seventh**	**Eighth**
31 days	30 days	31 days	30 days
Ninth	**Tenth**	**Eleventh**	**Twelfth**
31 days	30 days	31 days	30 days

Augustus Caesar's calendar, 7 B.C.

First	Second	Third	Fourth
31 days	28 days	31 days	30 days
Fifth	**Sixth**	**Seventh**	**Eighth**
31 days	30 days	31 days	31 days
Ninth	**Tenth**	**Eleventh**	**Twelfth**
30 days	31 days	30 days	31 days

The moon

Draw a picture of your skyline
on a sheet of paper.
Draw the position of the moon
each hour in relation to the skyline.
Record the time of each drawing.
Record the date.

Repeat this observation each night.
If you see the moon during the
day, mark it on your sheet.
Where does the moon rise and set?

Record the times when the moon
is full.
How long is it between one full
moon and the next?

Switch on a torch in a
darkened room.
Ask a friend to move a
white ball in an arc
through the torch beam.
Can you see the phases
of the moon on your
white ball?

Look up tide times.
Record the times of
neap tides and spring
tides.
Compare these with the
times of the full moon.
What pattern do you
notice?

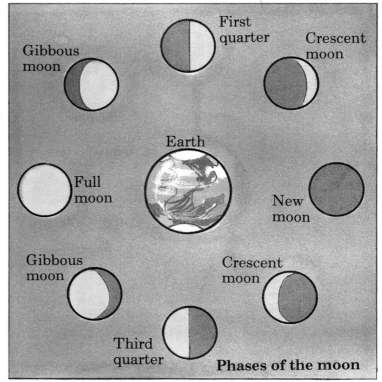

Phases of the moon

29

Speed

Speed is the time taken to travel a certain distance.
How long does it take you and your friend to run 100 metres?
How far can you and your friend run in 1 minute?

Make two marks on the roadside, a known distance apart.
Ask your friend to stand level with the
first mark. You stand level with the
second mark.
Ask your friend to wave a handkerchief
when a car passes his mark.
Measure the time from the moment you
see the handkerchief move until the car
passes your mark.
How long did it take the car to travel
between the marks?
How fast was the car travelling?

We measure speed at sea in knots.
Knots are the number of nautical miles
travelled in one hour.
A nautical mile is $\frac{1}{60}$ of 1° of longitude,
which is the same as $\frac{1}{60}$ of 1° of arc of the Earth's surface.

To measure star distances, we use the speed of light, which is
300,000,000 metres per second.
The sun is 8 light seconds away. How far is this?
Star distances are measured in light years, or the distance which
light travels in one year.
A light year is 300,000,000 metres x 60 seconds x 60 minutes x
24 hours x 365 days, which is 9,460,800,000,000 kilometres, or
5,878,940,000,000 miles.
Alpha Centauri, the nearest star to our solar system, is $4\frac{1}{3}$ light
years away from the Earth.
How far is Alpha Centauri from us, in kilometres or miles?

Chapter 4 Biological clocks

Rhythms

Most seashore plants and animals are affected by tides.
Many animals, such as sea anemones, barnacles, sea worms and periwinkles, feed on the incoming tide. The next time you visit the seashore, try to observe tidal feeding rhythms.

Many flowers only open in sunlight and close at night. Are there any plants like this in your area?
Listen for the birds' dawn chorus.
Which birds can you recognize?
Listen to the chorus over several days.
What pattern can you hear?
Which birds do you know that feed during the day?
Which birds feed at night?
These are daily rhythms.

What differences can you list in your local plants between winter and summer?
What reasons can you think of to account for these differences?
How do plants prepare for winter?
How do plants prepare for summer?
Plants use the shortening daylight hours to prepare for winter, and the lengthening hours to prepare for summer.
How do animals prepare for winter?
This is an annual rhythm.

Human biological clocks

Time your pulse over 1 minute.
What happens to your pulse after you run?
How many times do you breathe in a minute?
How many times do you breathe in a
minute after running?
Notice how your body timing adjusts to changes.

Hold a ruler vertically between your
finger and thumb.
Release your ruler and catch it again.
Record the distance that your ruler falls
before you catch it. Try this several times.
What happens?
Do this experiment with your other hand.
What happens? Notice how you can
improve with practice. Your body is
learning to improve its reaction time.

Record the times at which you eat each day.
Record your sleeping and waking times.
Record these times over a week.
How do you feel if you miss a meal or eat late?
How do you feel if you alter the times that you sleep?

Look at an airline timetable in a travel agency.
How long does it take to fly from London to New York?
At what time will you arrive? (See page 26.)
When will you go to sleep in New York?
Work out a journey which crosses the International Date Line.
How long does this journey take? When will you arrive?
After your arrival, when will your body want to sleep?
Crossing time zones causes jet lag.